P9-CRJ-568

THE ROO

A NATION'S ICON

Photography: Steve Parish

Text: Karin Cox

Steve Parish™
PUBLISHING

THE
ROO
A NATION'S ICON

contents

LEFT: Red Kangaroo silhouettes. TITLE PAGE: Eastern Grey Kangaroo.
PAGES 2–3: Eastern Grey Kangaroos at play.

introduction

Curious in composition, strangely elegant in locomotion and, in some cases, abundant in distribution, kangaroos and their relatives are truly unique to the Australian landscape. No other group of creatures embodies the virtues of this nation quite so successfully. Roos are hardy and enduring, making the most of Australia's boom or bust environments. They are also peaceful, yet convincing pugilists if provoked. Playful, comical, leisurely and social, they are synonymous with Australia's land, people and culture.

I have spent many hours watching kangaroos, and am always astonished by their individuality, their swiftness, their intelligence and their subtlety. With the twitch of an ear and the thump of a tail, my bounding photographic quarry is off — flying across the plains, over rocks or through bushland. It is no surprise to me that the "roo" has been chosen as a standard bearer for our Coat of Arms. It is an animal that leaves the most indelible impression both on Australians and on visitors from around the world.

This book has been motivated by two factors — firstly, to promote a broader understanding of the diversity of macropod species and their behaviours, and secondly, to provide a voice on behalf of all macropods: they certainly need one. Even though we idolise these amazing creatures, we have contributed to the demise of six species since European settlement and we are well on our way to eliminating several more. Greater understanding and education can help us avoid further extinction.

Steve Parish

LEFT: Kangaroos are inquisitive and alert animals. This male Red Kangaroo is cautiously investigating a disturbance in the grasslands.

Australia – a kangaroo culture

Since time immemorial, Indigenous Australians have found kangaroos perfectly suited to human needs — warm fur; easily replicated movements for dance; bone, teeth and claws for ceremonial dress; tender, tasty meat and a rapidly replenishing population. Europeans, initially perplexed by these bounding, boundless macropods, soon also came to recognise the beauty of these animals. Today, the image of the "roo" proliferates, depicted in the nation's sacred rock art sites, on our Coat of Arms, coins, airline, caps, flags and other tourist trinkets. Terms and titles such as "kangaroo court", *Skippy the Bush Kangaroo*, *Dot and the Kangaroo*, and the "boxing kangaroo" are ingrained in our language, literature, art and culture.

LEFT: Aborigines have long revered kangaroos and wallabies in rock art. This artwork in Kakadu National Park probably represents an Antilopine Wallaroo.

ABOVE: Kangaroos are integral to many ceremonial rites of Australian Aboriginal groups. Artwork, dances and songs record creation myths and moral stories, such as "The Woman Who Changed into a Kangaroo", which relays the tale of a woman's bizarre transformation upon running away from her responsibilities to her husband and children.

Indigenous **tales** and **totems**

An ancient bond exists between Australian Aborigines and kangaroos — a bond reflected in the many rock art depictions and legends relating to kangaroos and wallabies. Traditionally, macropods provided game, food and clothing, but they also played an important role in the pantheon of Dreaming spirits. Creation tales such as "How the Kangaroo Got its Long Tail", and the origin of the Kangaroo Dance are passed from generation to generation. Given its cultural significance, it is not surprising that the word kangaroo — derived from *ganjurru* in the Guugu Yimidhirr language — was one of the first Indigenous words to make its way into the English lexicon.

ABOVE: **Indigenous people retain the right to hunt their traditional quarry, which is then roasted over hot coals in an open fire. The skin and fur are left on.**

a contemporary **symbol** of Australia

European Australians quickly adopted this energetic bounding, boxing animal as a national mascot. Kangaroos and wallabies populate much of the continent, and their ubiquitous images feature heavily as logos and on tourist merchandise across the country. Along with being the standard-bearer on our Coat of Arms, the kangaroo winked cheekily at the sports-loving public as the giant-sized Matilda in the 1982 Commonwealth Games, travelled the world as the tail banner on our national carrier, boxed the air gleefully from the mast as *Australia II* snatched the America's Cup, and leapt into our currency on the fifty-cent and one-dollar coins.

ABOVE: The Red Kangaroo supports one side of the shield that makes up the Australian Coat of Arms. RIGHT: Tourist outlets and businesses capitalise on the cult of the roo.

AUSTRALIAN MADE

Brisbane

KANGAROOS
NEXT
10 km

$16.99

... THE GHOST
WHO HOPS ...

AUSTRALIA
Souvenir Gift Sets

The fame of the iconic roo is so widespread that visitors to Australia almost expect to see macropod marsupials bouncing along the airport's tarmac. QANTAS symbol aside, few roos are to be found around city airports, but many of Australia's State capitals have fulfilled the desire for city sightings by commissioning elaborate sculptures of roo species in the heart of public places.

LEFT: **Artist Christopher Trotter used scrap metal to create the intriguing *City Roos* in George St, Brisbane.**
RIGHT: **Macropods in the metropolis — Joan Walsh-Smith and Charles Smith fashioned these bronze roos near Stirling Gardens, Perth.**

living with roos

Many Australians "foster" orphaned or injured joeys — a commitment that can sometimes end up lasting a lifetime. Like all babies, joeys need nurturing, care and regular feeding, but they also require something harder to replicate — a warm, cosy pouch. Wildlife carers often use discarded pillow slips or slings to recreate this marsupial essential.

LEFT: Males, such as Dougal the Red Kangaroo, can become quite a handful as they mature. ABOVE, LEFT AND RIGHT: Licensed wildlife carers foster joeys (such as this Eastern Grey Kangaroo and Red-necked Wallaby) until they can be released into the wild. Wildlife sanctuaries often provide care for the duration of the animal's life.

ABOVE: Western Grey Kangaroos are gregarious, social animals that quickly become accustomed to humans.

Manicured golf courses, sports fields and school ovals are attractive habitats for mobs of Eastern and Western Grey Kangaroos. Humans have greatly increased the range of some kangaroo species, enticing them further inland to dams, lakes and crop fields, or encouraging a relaxed seaside existence near campgrounds on the coast. In these places, grey kangaroos come into close contact with humans and spend much time lolling in the shade, rarely moving unless someone threatens them. Despite their ease in the company of their mammalian kin, kangaroos should not be approached in the wild.

ABOVE: Eastern Grey Kangaroos create a pleasant diversion on the golf green.

Sanctuaries, zoos and wildlife parks usually promise safe, close-up encounters with Australia's kangaroo and wallaby species. The majority of macropod residents in wildlife parks are orphaned joeys that have been raised in captivity and readily return the affection given to them by wildlife staff and visitors.

OPPOSITE: A beachside clearing in Murramarang National Park, New South Wales, attracts an amiable contingent of Eastern Grey Kangaroos. TOP: Campers and visitors are often lucky enough to be approached by curious kangaroos eager for human attention. ABOVE: Kangaroos on show at Currumbin Wildlife Sanctuary, Queensland.

Most macropods are naturally inquisitive. Here, a campsite on Kangaroo Island, South Australia, and a magpie arouse the curiosity of a Western Grey Kangaroo.

ABOVE: Watching you watching me — a curious Whiptail Wallaby provides a photographer with a detailed close-up.

meet the macropods

Australia's macropods are a multifarious, highly individual mob united by hard-to-determine taxonomic links. Fifty-six Australian "macropod" species in three marsupial families are recognised under the superfamily group Macropodoidea, which loosely translates as "big-footed" animals and includes bettongs and potoroos, hare-wallabies, wallaroos and the larger, more commonly encountered, kangaroos and wallabies. Species exhibit a diversity of form, colour and character that sometimes makes identifying roos, especially from a distance or in poor light, a game of careful investigation and elimination. Differences, or similarities, in appearance and behaviour have at times led to confusion, with researchers proclaiming variant macropods a new species, or failing to recognise two distinct species. Until 1966, two of Australia's most common roos, Western and Eastern Greys, suffered from mistaken taxonomy. Up until their different gestation periods were confirmed, researchers believed them to be the same species.

LEFT: Red Kangaroos (*Macropus rufus*). Even within the same species, individuals are unique in feature, expression and personality. Some large males are aggressively dominant, disdainfully glowering when threatened — others are placid, curious or timid.

CLOCKWISE FROM TOP LEFT: Short-eared Rock-wallaby (*Petrogale brachyotis*); Proserpine Rock-wallaby (*Petrogale persephone*); Allied Rock-wallaby (*Petrogale assimilis*); Brush-tailed Rock-wallaby (*Petrogale penicillata*); Monjon (*Petrogale burbidgei*); Nabarlek, (*Petrogale concinna*); Rothschild's Rock-wallaby (*Petrogale rothschildi*); Mareeba Rock-wallaby (*Petrogale mareeba*); Unadorned Rock-wallaby (*Petrogale inornata*).

the rock-wallabies

Fleet of foot and small of stature, rock-wallabies are specialists of the mountains and stone country. Spring-loaded hindquarters equip these nimble creatures with a powerful bounce, allowing them to scale sheer cliff faces and disappear between crevices. Their thick-soled feet provide traction over slippery terrain and their muscular tails act as the aerial equivalent of a rudder. A high degree of adaptation to very particular environments, separated by distance or farmlands, has led to distinct colonies of rock-wallaby species and has, sadly, left some isolated species endangered.

ABOVE, LEFT TO RIGHT: Yellow-footed Rock-wallaby (*Petrogale xanthopus*); Black-footed Rock-wallaby (*Petrogale lateralis*); Purple-necked Rock-wallaby (*Petrogale purpureicollis*).

ABOVE, LEFT TO RIGHT: Northern Nailtail Wallaby (*Onychogalea unguifera*);
Bridled Nailtail Wallaby (*Onychogalea fraenata*).

the nailtail wallabies

Timid nailtail wallabies are an unfortunate casualty of Australia's European occupation. Three species once graced Australia's semi-arid shrublands and woodlands, but competition with feral arrivals, habitat destruction and a natural tendency to hide rather than run to escape predators has seen one species become extinct and rendered another, the Bridled Nailtail Wallaby, endangered. Their peculiar way of holding their forearms out in front, where they flap in small circles as they hop, led to the nickname "organ-grinders".

ABOVE: **John Gould's meticulously detailed artwork of the now extinct Crescent Nailtail Wallaby (*Oychogalea lunata*) records a species that was last sighted in 1964.** LEFT: **A close-up of the "nail" on the tail's end that earned this group of wallabies the moniker "nailtail". Despite being distinctive, this feature appears to have no biological function.**

CLOCKWISE FROM TOP LEFT: The species name of the Long-nosed Potoroo (*Potorous tridactylus*) came from the incorrect belief that the animal had only three toes; Long-footed Potoroo (*Potorous longipes*); Gilbert's Potoroo (*Potorous gilbertii*), believed extinct after vanishing for more than 100 years, was "rediscovered" in Two Peoples Bay Nature Reserve, Western Australia, in 1994.

the
potoroos

Small, omnivorous potoroos and their bettong and rat-kangaroo cousins retain some of the features of their ancient mammalian ancestors. Unlike other macropods, they build nests for reproductive purposes and use their weakly prehensile tails to gather nesting materials. Potoroos also have gourmet appetites. They forage for fungi and use their excellent olfactory sense to find highly sought-after truffles.

BELOW: **Unfortunately, Australia has the most appalling record of mammal extinctions in the world. The Broad-faced Potoroo (*Potorous platyops*) is one of at least 20 species lost to history.**

CLOCKWISE FROM TOP LEFT: Northern Bettong (*Bettongia tropica*); Brush-tailed Bettong (*Bettongia penicillata*); Burrowing Bettong (*Bettongia lesueur*); Musky Rat-kangaroo (*Hypsiprymnodon moschatus*); Southern Bettong (*Bettongia gaimardi*); Rufous Bettong (*Aepyprymnus rufescens*).

bettongs & the musky rat-kangaroo

Five living bettong species inhabit the Australian continent, but only one of them, the Rufous Bettong, appears to have escaped the ill-effects of human contact; all others have significantly declined in population. A fascinating relative is the Musky Rat-kangaroo — believed to be the most primitive of macropods, with a possible lineage to possum-like ancestors. Among macropods, the Musky Rat-kangaroo is the only species in which giving birth to twins is a common occurrence.

ABOVE: **The extinct Desert Rat-kangaroo (*Caloprymnus campestris*), in a drawing by naturalist John Gould, once inhabited gibber-strewn desert and aridland plains in South Australia and Queensland. No specimens have been recorded since 1935.**

the hare-wallabies

Perfectly adapted to life in harsh conditions, these compact, water-efficient animals occupy Australia's arid and semi-aridlands where they seek refuge from the sun's strength in hollows in the earth, tunnels in tussock grass or in shallow burrows. Two among their number have been lost to the world, and two more, the Rufous Hare-wallaby and Banded Hare-wallaby, are now confined to a limited range on Bernier and Dorre Islands off Western Australia. Despite its similar appearance, the Banded Hare-wallaby is believed to be only a distant relative of the other hare-wallabies, being the sole surviving member of its otherwise extinct subfamily, the Sthenurinae.

OPPOSITE, CLOCKWISE FROM TOP: Spectacled Hare-wallaby (*Lagorchestes conspicillatus*); Rufous Hare-wallaby (*Lagorchestes hirsutus*); Banded Hare-wallaby (*Lagostrophus fasciatus*). ABOVE: The Eastern Hare-wallaby (*Lagorchestes leporides*) is now presumed extinct along with Central Hare-wallaby (*Lagorchestes asomatus*). The Central Hare-wallaby is Australia's most mysterious macropod. Its complete skeleton has never been recovered — the species is known only from Indigenous accounts and a single skull.

the tree-kangaroos

The most likely evolutionary path for kangaroos was from arboreal, possum-like animals to terrestrial kangaroos and wallabies. Only one group, comprised of two native species, has sought to reverse that order by returning to a life in the treetops. Curiously, tree-kangaroo evolution has not favoured the re-aquisition of all of the attributes designed for arboreal life. While they have opposable thumbs, rough-soled feet to secure a firm grip, and the ability to move their hind legs independently (a trait exclusive to this macropod group), their tails are not prehensile like those of many other arboreal animals. Instead, tree-kangaroos use their long, heavy tails as a counterweight. They are deft operators in the treetops, moving with perfect balance through the forest canopy in the hunt for tender leaves and fruit.

LEFT AND OPPOSITE: **The continent's largest arboreal mammal is Bennett's Tree-kangaroo (*Dendrolagus bennettianus*) which enjoys a nocturnal existence in pockets of tropical vine forest in Queensland's north.** ABOVE: **Lumholtz's Tree-kangaroo (*Dendrolagus lumholtzi*) is somewhat smaller and survives only in highland rainforest between Mount Spurgeon and Cardwell in Queensland.**

the swamp wallaby

The Swamp Wallaby is another marsupial original. In zoological terms, it is the only true "wallaby" — the sole member of the genus *Wallabia*. It is distinguished from its kin by its darker fur, diurnal habits, larger premolar teeth and unusual gait. When moving at pace, the Swamp Wallaby's head stays low to the ground while its tail extends rigidly behind, giving it a "greyhound-like" appearance.

ABOVE: **A joey too large for the pouch will be physically ejected by its mother. This is achieved by simply leaning forward. It is at this stage in a joey's life that it is most vulnerable to predators.**

the quokka

Stout, adorable Quokkas — also the only species of their genus — had a hand in the naming of Western Australia's Rottnest Island, where populations flourish. Navigator Willem de Vlamingh mistook the small marsupials on the island for large rodents, naming the place "Rat Nest Island", or *Rottenest* in his native Dutch. Fortunately, there is nothing at all rat-like about the Quokka; nor do they build nests, being in possession of comfortable pouches for young.

BELOW: **Quokkas are endemic to Western Australia and are most prolific on Rottnest Island. Populations, however, are increasing in some habitats on the mainland.**

the pademelons

Pademelons are shy, forest fringe-dwellers. These crepuscular marsupials emerge tentatively in the still of the evening or early morning to graze on grassy patches at the edge of the forest. If a group of pademelons becomes suddenly alarmed, alert heads spring up like jack-in-the-boxes, ears swivelling, before the mob retreats with short, bouncy hops to the shelter of the forest's darker recesses. Quiet observers may be lucky enough to earn an audience with these careful creatures.

OPPOSITE: Red-necked Pademelon (*Thylogale thetis*).
ABOVE, LEFT TO RIGHT: Tasmanian Pademelon (*Thylogale billardierii*); Red-legged Pademelon (*Thylogale stigmatica*).

ABOVE, LEFT TO RIGHT: In the 1960s, the Parma Wallaby (*Macropus parma*) teetered on the brink of extinction — individuals were repatriated from New Zealand to save this vulnerable wallaby species; The remarkable Tammar Wallaby (*Macropus eugenii*) is perfectly adapted for island life and can quench its thirst on seawater; The Red-necked Wallaby (*Macropus rufogriseus*) has a Tasmanian subspecies *Macropus rufogriseus rufogriseus,* which is known as Bennett's Wallaby.

medium-sized wallabies & wallaroos

Sharing the same genus as the larger kangaroos (*Macropus*), wallabies and wallaroos are some of the continent's most commonly seen roos. Like kangaroos, most wallabies feed and live in small mobs, but the wallaby's distinguishing features include generally weighing less than 25 kilograms, while wallaroos can be identified by a black nose and a tendency to occupy rugged, hilly terrain.

LEFT: Delicately featured, and with a marked line decorating the face, the Whiptail Wallaby (*Macropus parryi*) is occasionally known as the Pretty-face Wallaby.
ABOVE: One of the continent's "most beautiful and elegant" wallabies, as described by Frederic Wood Jones in 1924, was the Toolache Wallaby (*Macropous greyi*). Sadly, later that same year, the Toolache disappeared entirely. Its attractively patterned coat, a popular target for hunters and fur traders, only hastened the extinction of this species.

ABOVE, LEFT TO RIGHT: Western Brush Wallaby (*Macropus irma*); Agile Wallaby (*Macropus agilis*); Black-striped Wallaby (*Macropus dorsalis*).

ABOVE, LEFT TO RIGHT: Black Wallaroo (*Macropus bernardus*); Common Wallaroo (*Macropus robustus*); Antilopine Wallaroo (*Macropus antilopinus*).

big
kangaroos

Easily the most engaging macropods, and those that have become the most firmly ensconced in Australian culture, are the larger roos. These masters of drought and distance are able to travel quickly over some of Australia's harshest country, using speed, endurance and a power-packed kick to defeat predators. Between them, the Eastern Grey, Western Grey and Red Kangaroo occupy much of the continent.

OPPOSITE, LEFT TO RIGHT: Western Grey Kangaroo (*Macropus fuliginosus*); Eastern Grey Kangaroo (*Macropus giganteus*); Red Kangaroo (*Macropus rufus*). ABOVE: Despite their seemingly innocuous appearance, roos (especially dominant males) are just as equipped for fight as they are for flight. Balancing on a strong tail, they can launch powerful kicks with their hind legs and may even disembowel predators, rival males or intrusive humans.

places
to live

One of the traits that adds to the roo's totemic appeal is its stoic resilience. They are hardy occupiers of habitat and are widely distributed, ranging from Australia's arid heartlands to the craggy highlands, tropical rainforest and arable farmlands that fringe the continent's coast. Human settlement has variably affected macropod species. Some, especially the larger roos, have benefited from the increase in food and water created by agriculture. Dams, bores, irrigation and crop fields sustain species in times when they would otherwise decline. Other species have been forced into the habitable corners of densely populated areas, or driven away from developed areas that were once part of their range. Over time, each species has adapted to those environments that provide for its physical, reproductive and behavioural needs, adjusting to any habitat that will give the animal its best chance of survival.

OPPOSITE, CLOCKWISE FROM TOP LEFT: **Various habitats support one or more of the macropod species — Red Kangaroo; Rufous Hare-wallaby; Yellow-footed Rock-wallaby; Long-nosed Potoroo; Western Grey Kangaroo; Common Wallaroo; Rufous Bettong; Eastern Grey Kangaroo; Lumholtz's Tree-kangaroo.** LEFT, TOP TO BOTTOM: **Swamp Wallabies prefer dense understoreys or grassy tussocks where they can hide if necessary; Logs and debris of the open forests and woodlands camouflage the muted colours of most species; Quokkas gather around freshwater soaks.**

temperate & cool woodlands & wet forests

With their tall gums and an understorey of abundant grasses, ferns and groundcover, woodlands and wet sclerophyll forests are fitting homes for larger macropods as well as some of the smaller, shyer species. Reclusive pademelons creep out to feed on grassy areas that abut wet forests, retreating to the fern-filled understorey when alarmed. Larger roos of the woodlands find safety in numbers, living in mobs that maximise the number of eyes and ears alert to possible danger.

LEFT: Eastern Grey Kangaroos congregate in mobs in the woodlands.
ABOVE: The Red-necked Pademelon prefers the sanctuary of rainforest and wet eucalypt forest, making grazing forays onto grassy patches at the edge of the forest.

temperate & cool
grasslands

Spacious grasslands offer fresh green pick after rain or wildfire, but provide little in the way of shelter. Individuals in these wide-open spaces usually gather in mobs for protection and are mostly sizable enough to make a swift escape should danger threaten. Scarcity of food during drought, flood or inclement snowy weather may force macropods to go "on the hop" in search of greener pastures.

ABOVE: **Vulnerable Eastern Grey Kangaroos keep a few sentinels on lookout at all times.** RIGHT: **A furry winter coat protects the Red-necked Wallaby from snow.**

tropical open woodlands & grasslands

Nature has a remarkably fine eye for colour-matching. In the tropical open grasslands and savannas the sienna and sepia tones of dry grass and speckled bark are matched by the camouflaging coats of grassland inhabitants. Stealth and silence are crucial weapons in the arsenal of tropical macropods. When threatened, Antilopine Wallaroos will freeze stock-still before taking off at speed. Smaller macropods, like the diminutive hare-wallabies, use their size to maintain a low profile in the undergrowth.

OPPOSITE: Northern Nailtail Wallaby. LEFT: Spectacled Hare-wallaby. ABOVE: Antilopine Wallaroos usually live in small mobs and feed on grass in the late afternoon.

tropical rainforests

Macropods find all manner of delicacies in the rainforest larder — so much so that some have reverted to an arboreal lifestyle where they can feast at leisure on the rainforest's botanical bounty of fruit and tender leaves. Forest fruit is a powerful attractant, but most ground-dwelling species here have surprisingly diverse appetites, supplementing their diet with invertebrates, tubers, and fungi, which flourish in the moist rainforest.

OPPOSITE, TOP TO BOTTOM: Lush tropical rainforests support several macropod species; The Musky Rat-kangaroo is a ground-dwelling connoisseur of fungi, fruit, seeds and insects in rainforests between Ingham and Cooktown. ABOVE, LEFT TO RIGHT: Lumholtz's Tree-kangaroo has evolved an arboreal lifestyle; Red-legged Pademelon.

tropical stone country

Rock-wallabies are the undisputed rulers of the craggy fortresses that rise from Australia's stone country, although the Black Wallaroo also appreciates the protection afforded by sheer spires and slabs of exfoliating rock. High vantage points, subtle colours, keen senses and supple physiques usually allow stone country residents to notice trespassers to their domain well before they themselves are apparent.

OPPOSITE, CLOCKWISE FROM TOP: Rugged formations make protective homes for rock-hopping macropods; Allied Rock-wallaby; Black Wallaroo; Mareeba Rock-wallaby. ABOVE: A Short-eared Rock-wallaby keeps watch.

coastal sandy heathlands

The structure and composition of underlying rock, and the sediments and sands that accumulate upon it, are the foundations of habitat. These factors determine the plants that thrive in a particular region, which in turn attract animals that find in that environment the fulfilment of their lifestyle needs. Consequently, it is not surprising that the sandy soiled, densely shrubbed coastal heathlands invite smaller macropods that are suited to digging and hiding, along with the common and more robust Eastern Grey Kangaroo. Efficient water conservation (a physiological feature of the Banded Hare-wallaby, which does not drink) is another trait strongly favoured in this habitat.

LEFT: Twilight envelops coastal scrub in Wilsons Promontory National Park and further camouflages the coat of an Eastern Grey Kangaroo. BELOW, LEFT TO RIGHT: Soft sandy soils yield edible roots and fungi for the Banded Hare-wallaby and Long-nosed Potoroo.

ABOVE: Swamp Wallaby habitat, such as that of North Stradbroke Island in Queensland, must include plenty of cover to shelter a macropod that is more diurnal than most.

ABOVE: Contrary to its name, the Swamp Wallaby exploits various habitats. It is the largest animal of the coastal heath environment and lives alone, foraging on grasses and ferns.

ABOVE: A Western Grey Kangaroo surveys the sparse landscape. LEFT TO RIGHT: The Burrowing Bettong survives on four Western Australian islands and has been re-introduced in South Australia; Efforts to re-establish populations of Rufous Hare-wallabies in the Tanami Desert are under way. OPPOSITE: Red Kangaroos are masters of drought and are commonly found across all arid flatland habitats.

sandy & stony aridlands

Tracts of inhospitable desert, almost featureless but for runnels of wind-sculptured sand, seem unlikely habitats for mammals; however, a few hardy macropods find their niche in these desolate landscapes. Strategies that reduce energy and conserve water are mandatory. Larger species rest during the day and roam further afield to find nutritious patches when required. The smaller Rufous Hare-wallaby finds sufficient water in its diet, while the Burrowing Bettong, which has been re-introduced to the mainland under South Australia's Arid Recovery program, constructs an elaborate, cool warren system.

arid ranges & uplands

Similar conditions to the stone country habitat call for comparable adaptations and lifestyles. Wallabies of the mountainous, rocky aridlands rest during the day in the cool of caves or rock overhangs, coming out to feed on grass and leaves at night or in the cool of the evening. Rock-wallaby species share this habitat with the larger, stockier Common Wallaroo. Such unforgiving terrain is negotiated with the aid of thickly soled hindlimbs, which supply maximum traction on rocky surfaces.

LEFT: Common Wallaroos inhabit much of mainland Australia and often use the shelter of surrounding rocky ranges as a cool, well-protected base. ABOVE: The Black-footed Rock-wallaby can be distinguished by the coarse, rubbery black soles of its feet.

arid & semi-arid grassy woodlands

Patchy woodlands and plains, intermittently broken by low-growing brush and straggly scrub, provide habitat for the indomitable Red Kangaroo and widely distributed Common Wallaroo. Common Wallaroos are solitary creatures, while more sociable Red Kangaroos gather in mobs, usually with a dominant male protecting a small group of females. Both species can cover much ground in a single day if necessary, but are not naturally nomadic — moving only short distances in most cases. Longer journeys are usually only undertaken when arid environments become too harsh to sustain these species any longer.

LEFT: "Red Kangaroo" sometimes appears to be a misnomer, especially in the case of females, which often have a duller, grey-brown coat. ABOVE: In some parts of its extensive range, the Common Wallaroo is referred to as the "Euro".

roo
lifestyles

Macropods are relatively diverse in size, colour, form and habitat, but behaviour is just as variable. However many common threads bind macropod behaviour, it is the singular differences that add character and mark individuality. Most species are almost wholly nocturnal, inconspicuously going about their business by moonlight; those that are not prefer twilight or dawn wanderings. Few, with the exception perhaps of the Quokka, can be said to be truly diurnal. Some species are highly gregarious, forming hierarchical bonds within a mob; others prefer the ease of movement afforded by a solitary life. All give birth to live young that are nurtured on milk in a forwards-facing pouch, but gestation times vary and one species (the Musky Rat-kangaroo) differs in routinely producing twins. Species may share similarly keen senses of hearing, smell and sight, and display recognisable reproductive, nurturing and defensive body language, but the delight for roo lovers is in the fleeting, personal expressions that make each animal, and its life, uniquely precious.

LEFT: The rising orb of the moon silhouettes a gathering of nocturnal macropods.

sensitive hearing

Large, independently swivelling ears give some macropods an endearing, comical appearance, but these body parts are also powerful defences against predation. Roos can detect sounds of many frequencies, including the gentle foot-thumping of a concerned mob mate. Such auditory sensitivity has led to attempts to control kangaroo populations by using devices that emit deterrent noises to help keep roos away from crops or highways.

OPPOSITE: A cautious Common Wallaroo, with ears alert, peeps up from its rocky hiding place. ABOVE: The tentative ear twitchings of young Red-necked Wallabies.

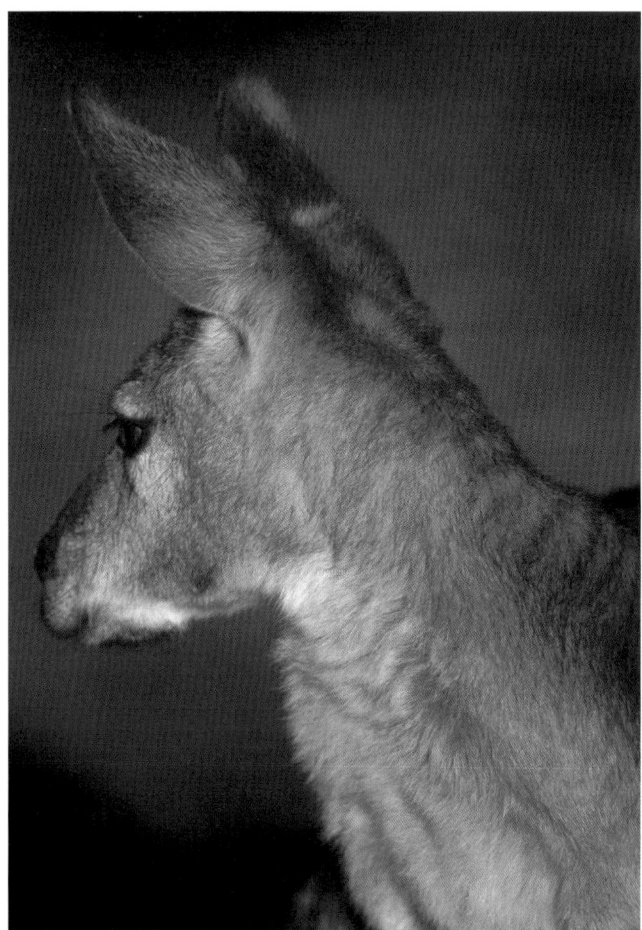

kangaroo vision

A kangaroo's hearing is keener than its eyesight, so most macropod species remain on constant auditory alert. Animals that live in large mobs appreciate the protection afforded by a changing "guard" that is constantly watching and listening for approaching danger. Regularly "surveying" — adopting a rigid posture, head raised and thumping feet at the ready — is an important task. For largely nocturnal mammals, sight improves under the cover of darkness and moving objects are more readily observed than stationary ones. If danger threatens, urgent grunts and stomps alert the mob.

OPPOSITE: A Swamp Wallaby gazes intently into the distance; Eastern Grey Kangaroo. ABOVE, CLOCKWISE FROM TOP LEFT: Taking "opposing views" is a popular strategy for enhancing vision and is commonly adopted by Red-necked Pademelons, Western Grey Kangaroos and Yellow-footed Rock Wallabies. Solitary species, such as the Common Wallaroo, survey from elevated positions, giving them a panoramic scope of their surrounds.

scenting

ABOVE: A male Western Grey Kangaroo smells a female. Any olfactory signs of a female entering her oestrous cycle will quickly be picked up by the male's nose. OPPOSITE: Scenting may also help alert roos to fire, predators, food and water.

Our human estimation of the power of smell is often underrated, especially compared to that of our wild mammalian relatives. In macropods, smell helps to detect friends, foes and fire; attract (or perhaps repel) a potential partner; and aid in the location of food and water. The fecundity of kangaroos and other macropods is well known, and mating occurs almost immediately after a joey is born, however females remain sexually receptive for just a few hours when they come into oestrus. A male's sense of smell is a useful paternal tool. Dominant males regularly monitor females, sniffing at the pouch and cloacal area to effectively pick up any faint aromas of macropod ardour.

hiding to survive

The combined senses of sight, hearing and smell often give roos a headstart on impending threats, yet their defensive behaviour may be even more crucial to their survival. In the choice between fight or flight, most prefer the latter, remaining true to their big-footed body shape. However, many smaller macropods simply don't have the stamina for a sustained chase; instead, they make a habit of concealment. Some habitats and some species are highly suited to this strategy — rock-wallabies, for instance, gain a distinct advantage by slipping into a crevice — and sometimes temporary cover, such as shrewd use of camouflage or retreating to a grass tussock, may be all that is required.

ABOVE: **A Short-eared Rock-wallaby withdraws to a rocky fissure.** OPPOSITE, LEFT TO RIGHT: **The Bridled Nailtail Wallaby's habit of running only a short distance before hiding has, unfortunately, almost led to its demise; An Eastern Grey finds camouflage in foliage.**

foraging & feeding

Macropod species have a range of dietary preferences. Many, especially rainforest species, are omnivorous, consuming fruit and insects with equal gusto. Others, such as bettongs and potoroos, favour fungi. Herbivorous species like kangaroos require digestive capabilities similar to ruminants (cattle, sheep etc.) in order to break down fibrous plant tissues. Typically, their gustatory endeavours are aided by two chisel-like lower incisors and six upper incisors that allow macropods to clip off plants, which are then masticated by grinding molars. The four molars on each side of the upper and lower jaw emerge slowly and move forward along the jaw as an animal gets older.

OPPOSITE, TOP TO BOTTOM: Feeding activity increases around dusk; Agile Wallabies exist on a diet of grass, fruit and leaves. ABOVE, LEFT TO RIGHT: A Whiptail Wallaby feasts on a palm nut kernel; Invertebrates, fungi and roots appeal to the Long-nosed Potoroo.

drinking

Water is essential to animal survival, but some of this continent's remarkable, arid-adapted mammals rarely need to drink; like the Koala, they ingest rather than imbibe — receiving liquid from food. Hare-wallabies, bettongs and the seawater-drinking Tammar Wallaby suffer few ill-effects from drought — a natural regime which can nevertheless prove disastrous for kangaroo, wallaby and rock-wallaby species. Luckily, agriculture has led to an increase of dams, weirs, cattle troughs and other sources of ground water, which has subsequently increased the population of some species.

ABOVE, LEFT TO RIGHT: **Unlike bettongs, potoroos (like this Long-nosed Potoroo) must drink; A Common Wallaroo slakes his thirst at a rocky stream. Studies of drinking behaviour around a New South Wales stock trough showed that, surprisingly, Common Wallaroos take dominance over larger Red Kangaroos near water. Who gets to drink first and for how long is usually determined by a size-related hierarchy within species.** OPPOSITE: **A female Eastern Grey Kangaroo with pouch young will sometimes enter the water to drink, especially in hot weather.**

a curious gait

Over-developed hindlimbs are extremely useful appendages for making airborne leaps over outback plains, but for more leisurely, everyday locomotion they prove cumbersome. Strangely, a quirk of the nervous system precludes most macropods from moving their back legs independently on land; however, tree-kangaroos and the Musky Rat-kangaroo can do so and, curiously, kangaroos swim using alternate kicks. Instead, most macropods undertake an awkward pentapedal "walk", balancing on the forelimbs and strong tail while simultaneously swinging the back legs forward.

ABOVE: The Eastern Grey Kangaroo's tail acts as its fifth appendage.
RIGHT: A Western Brush Wallaby, like all of its relatives, employs its tail as a "leg" to give it balance when moving forward.

on the hop

On marathon journeys, a roo's muscular legs are truly unbeatable. At less then 6 kilometres an hour, larger roos adopt a clumsy pentapedal walk, but when they feel the need for speed, hopping is far and away the most efficient motion. Effortlessly bounding along at 15–25 kilometres an hour expends minimal energy for the distance covered. At a fixed hopping rate, elastic tendons reserve and reuse energy with each spring-loaded leap. Energy use increases with speed and stride length, but this doesn't stop roos from reaching a top speed of up to 64 kilometres an hour!

OPPOSITE AND ABOVE: Species can often be identified by subtle differences in their hopping style. The fastest species are the Eastern and Western Grey Kangaroos, Red Kangaroos, the Common Wallaroo and larger wallaby species such as the Whiptail Wallaby above.

ABOVE: A Red-necked Wallaby in full flight easily clears obstructions such as fallen logs. OPPOSITE, TOP TO BOTTOM: Southern Bettongs and other smaller macropods have a shorter stride than big kangaroos but are still speedy little hoppers; Some wallabies, such as this Bridled Nailtail Wallaby, have a lower, less bouncy carriage and lean forward when moving at pace.

ABOVE AND OPPOSITE: The Western Brush Wallaby is a shy, solitary wallaby restricted to South-West Western Australia. Even the slightest hint of danger will cause it to run at an alarming speed. It takes long strides, using its tail to provide the balance needed for making sudden turns. Here a yearling follows its mother at equal speed.

ABOVE: Red Kangaroos are the record holders when it comes to the highest leap. An astonished hunting party recorded that one frantic male Red Kangaroo bounded 3.1 metres heavenwards, easily clearing a stack of timber blocking its escape.

ABOVE: Obviously, snow and other slippery or precarious surfaces restrict the fluid movement of kangaroo and wallaby species, such as this Red-necked Wallaby. Luckily, Australia's snowy seasons are, for the most part, relatively short. Few species are forced to endure a snow-laden territory for the duration of winter.

fearless rock-hoppers

Grace and agility typify the rock-wallaby species, which can be seen effortlessly scaling cliffs and vaulting boulders in Australia's more mountainous climes. The long, flexible tail governs stability and steering, balancing the weight of the wallaby's body as it launches through the air.

ABOVE: Daring rock-wallabies, such as this Yellow-footed Rock-wallaby, regularly undertake enormous leaps from one cluster of well-worn rocks to another.

tactile
tree-climbers

Longer arms, opposable thumbs and formidable re-curved claws assist tree-kangaroos with their arboreal movements, yet these large mammals will never match the treetop dexterity of smaller marsupials like possums and gliders. Excellent grip and a tactile "hang on for dear life" approach, along with the ability to carefully walk backwards along branches, give these macropods their edge in the trees. Life in the rainforest canopy provides few competitors, abundant fruit and leaves and most of the tree-kangaroos' needs, so they rarely need to venture to the rainforest floor. When they do so, they slide down tail first, gripping the trunk with the forepaws before executing a gymnastic flip about 2 metres from the ground and landing upright.

RIGHT: **If frightened, tree-kangaroos can spring to the ground from a height of 15 metres. A more leisurely way to descend is tail first, as this Lumholtz's Tree-kangaroo is demonstrating.**

tiny & timid excavators

Rather than attempt to outrun predators over land, the Burrowing Bettong has a subterranean strategy of evasion. Digging complex underground burrows makes sense for a species that routinely excavates to search for roots and tubers anyway. Other small macropods may fashion shallow hollows in the earth, but the Burrowing Bettong is the only macropod that lives a social life in warrens housing many individuals. Before the fox drove it to local extinction on the mainland, the Burrowing Bettong often shared its warrens with rabbits. It now survives in the wild only on Dorre, Bernier, Barrow and Boodie Islands off the Western Australian coast.

OPPOSITE AND ABOVE: Living in burrows is cooler and safer for the Burrowing Bettong.

night-time nest builders

Unlike the Burrowing Bettong, the Tasmanian, Northern, Rufous and Brush-tailed Bettongs all live above ground in specially constructed nests built of a combination of leaves, twigs and grasses over shallow depressions or under thick shrubs or grass-trees. They may construct several nests across their home range, and visit the nests randomly. Despite being solitary animals, bettongs have large home ranges (in excess of 20 hectares) that often intersect.

Truffles (fruiting bodies of underground fungi) appear to be the most important component of the bettong's diet. Bettongs also feed on a wide range of other foods, including a number of fungus species, roots, tubers, seeds, insects, grass and leaves.

Bettongs are nocturnal, sleeping during the day in their well-concealed nests. Unfortunately, these nests afford little protection from predators. All species live under constant threat from foxes, feral cats and Dingoes.

OPPOSITE: During the day a female Rufous Bettong and her joey will hide in their bush nest, emerging at night to feed. ABOVE: Recorded an hour before dawn, this nest-building Brush-tailed Bettong began gathering grass in its prehensile tail.

communicating the kangaroo way

The 1960s television show *Skippy the Bush Kangaroo* popularised the charming but baseless idea that kangaroos could communicate through a series of tic-like "tsks" (and even make themselves understood to humans). In reality, kangaroos and wallabies have a number of vocalisations, which, combined with body language, allow them to get their message across. Patterns of communication and the sounds emitted are dependent on age, sex and situation. Isolated or abandoned joeys make sounds very different from those uttered by content juveniles. Guttural, almost growling sounds or hissing, accompanied by foot-thumping, usually signify danger or distress, while gentler grunts, sniffing, sneezing and nuzzling may be seen in maternal and sexual interaction.

RIGHT, TOP TO BOTTOM: When caught exposed and unawares, the Short-eared Rock-wallaby may exhibit signs of surprise or stress such as stiffness, a frozen expression, foot-thumping or vocalisations; A male Quokka spends a great deal of time "connecting" with his harem of females: the connection can be as simple as rubbing noses.

Kangaroo courtship is also governed by specific behaviour, such as tail scratching, sniffing and tail arching. When females consent to mate they raise their tails, encouraging the male to mount. Ambivalent or extremely submissive behaviour may indicate fear or reluctance on the part of the female.

ABOVE: A mature male Black-striped Wallaby shows an obvious carnal interest in a much younger and seemingly reticent female. RIGHT: Panting may be a sign that a macropod is hot or in distress. Kangaroos do not sweat, so panting and forearm licking help keep them cool. Both of these behaviours can sometimes also be observed when roos are nervous.

communicating

ABOVE: Natural threat responses for most macropods are either to appear invincible by flexing muscles and drawing up to full height or, if the opposition is too strong, to show submission, cower or flee. Males, females and even juveniles display such behaviour depending on the anxiety they feel, as seen in the postures of this Red-necked Wallaby juvenile and male adult. OPPOSITE, CLOCKWISE FROM LEFT: An Eastern Grey Kangaroo prepares to face a threat; The sensitive Western Brush Wallaby communicates nervousness by wriggling its long tail or lashing it from side to side, usually as a precursor to taking flight.

kangaroo camps

During the heat of the day most roos are at rest, conserving their energy for nocturnal forays or social twilight gatherings. In the woodlands and forests, larger roos and wallabies may scratch out a shallow hollow in the earth — most choose locations with groundcover that camouflages their coat, or else camp close to the safety of sheltering brush. When comfortably reclined under a River Red Gum or surrounded by clumps of shrubbery, they are reluctantly disturbed, preferring to laze, lounge and watch the day grow long.

ABOVE AND OPPOSITE: Although some species are marginally diurnal and may be seen on the move during the day, lazing in a kangaroo camp is usually the preferred daytime activity for the Western Grey Kangaroo (above) and Red Kangaroo (opposite).

keeping cool

Marsupials that dwell in Australia's sweltering environments must find ways to keep their cool, even when the mercury rises above 40° C. Macropods and potoroids do not sweat, so heat management requires different means, such as panting, licking the forearms and exposing less densely furred body surfaces to the air. A network of veins runs under the thin skin on a kangaroo's forelimbs; when licked, blood flow increases and the evaporating saliva cools the blood. Roos may also pull the tail between the legs, spread-eagle themselves, or scratch the ground to throw up cool, sub-surface dirt.

OPPOSITE, TOP TO BOTTOM: **Digging a cool, shallow pit and stretching out help keep a Red Kangaroo cool.** ABOVE: **Forearm licking cools the blood and reduces heat. A drawback in dry environments, however, is the loss of body fluid.**

warming up

Much of Australia experiences warm to hot weather for large parts of the year, but even tropical and desert climates cool considerably at night and during winter. Macropods are widely distributed and cold weather warm-up strategies must be used on occasion, both in the north and in cooler southern regions. Rock-wallabies have ideal solutions for heat and cold, avoiding the heat by sheltering in cool recesses and warding off cold by lolling on sun-warmed rocks. Basking is not exclusively a reptilian practice; mammals, from roos to humans, also enjoy a spot of sunbathing to warm up and wind down.

OPPOSITE: After a very cold night this female adult Quokka and its yearling soak up the warm rays of the sun. Quokkas may at first face the sun, then turn as a sunbathing human would, presenting their rear ends for a total warm up. ABOVE: Warm morning sun and a big yawn kick-start this Red-necked Wallaby's day.

fighting

Boxing and brawling, for which kangaroos are world famous, constitute either playful or fearful behaviour for roos. To learn this crucial defence mechanism, juveniles grapple, wrestle and cuff each other (or their long-suffering macropod mums). Fighting skills are especially vital for mature bucks, who seek to dominate siblings and former "joey-hood" friends in order to fulfil their biological urges and protect their domain from predators or other marauding males. Males may have biceps capable of packing a potent punch, but their true strength lies in mighty kicks delivered by the hindlimbs.

ABOVE: Two Agile Wallabies circle each other aggressively. When fighting, they may trade grunts, like boxers trading insults, before going a number of rounds, occasionally stopping to tear up and throw grass, or to scratch out "their turf".

LEFT: A bit of rough-and-tumble fun with roos of a similar age is a regular play act for joeys or juveniles. Later in life these games become much more serious. Social macropods that form mobs rely on the dominance of a boomer (or "alpha male") and only one buck will benefit from that superior position. Younger males must attempt to establish a similarly comfortable home life for themselves as they grow in size and fighting skill. Even species that prefer to travel alone find fighting skills essential when backed into a corner.

ABOVE: Female kangaroos know the importance of teaching their joeys how to stand on their own two feet — and tail! Mothers may playfully box as a form of education, and also discipline. This Eastern Grey Kangaroo mother is gently introducing her joey to the pugilistic craft.

ABOVE: An Eastern Grey Kangaroo instinctively adopts a defensive pose when startled by a Tasmanian Devil. In this position, the kangaroo protects its forearms from the Devil's nip while giving herself enough space to kick.

socialising

A few solitary species aside, macropods are for the most part gregarious and social mammals. For larger roos, mobs generally comprise about ten mostly related individuals, although in times of plenty much larger mobs will congregate in one area. To ensure social harmony, strict rules of hierarchy and etiquette are observed and relationships are maintained through play-fighting, mutual grooming and affection. Grooming, tail nibbling and back scratching are common favours granted to females by males seeking favours of a more amorous nature.

ABOVE, LEFT & RIGHT: A large mob of Eastern Grey Kangaroos, including many juveniles, grazes contentedly on fresh green grass; If danger threatens the peace and safety of the mob, they take flight, bounding away in unison and keeping juveniles well protected in the centre of the moving mob. OPPOSITE: An Antilopine Wallaroo nuzzles its offspring. By the time a joey is ready to leave the comfort of the pouch, it has formed a strong attachment to its mother and will continue to associate with her for some time after weaning.

ABOVE: Female Red-necked Wallabies — like most marsupials — make devoted, affectionate mothers, often caring for pouch young and yearlings simultaneously.

ABOVE: The nurturing bond between a maternal Whiptail Wallaby and her joey is evident in the loving body language between the two.

grooming & stretching

With such thick fur, personal hygiene clearly requires a fastidious and dedicated approach. Macropod paws are equipped with long claws that can penetrate the fluffy cloak, and flexible musculature allows them to scratch almost any itch. Incisors at the front of a kangaroo's mouth are also used to nip at offending burrs or tangles. Females find cleanliness even more important. In preparation for each tiny new arrival mothers must clean the nursery, nuzzling and licking the warm depths of the pouch.

OPPOSITE, LEFT TO RIGHT: An Agile Wallaby plumbs the depths of its dense fur; Even on watch, an Eastern Grey Kangaroo takes time out to enjoy a scratch. ABOVE, LEFT TO RIGHT: It's not such a stretch for a Red-necked Wallaby to make sure its tail is kept tidy; Females lick the inside of the pouch to keep it clean — even when a joey is in residence. When this female Swamp Wallaby finishes tidying one side, she will simply nudge the joey across with her nose in order to clean the other side.

courting & mating

Macropods are remarkably fertile. Dominant males enjoy a healthy sex life, seeking sexual favours from any number of females within their harems. Some of these females may already have a joey at heel and another in the pouch when they fall pregnant again. A dominant boomer is a busy fellow — each doe can demand a committed approach to courtship, in which case the male must indulge in roo foreplay for several days by regularly sniffing and nuzzling the cloaca or scratching his partner's tail. During this time, his potential partner may also frequently urinate on him — her urine and scent help him pinpoint her receptiveness. When consenting, she will arch her tail — a cue that lets the male know she is ready to mate.

OPPOSITE: **A female Eastern Grey may come into oestrus while she still has a joey in the pouch.** ABOVE: **The buck's curving, s-shaped (sigmoid) penis penetrates the doe from behind, while the female's young is still in the pouch.**

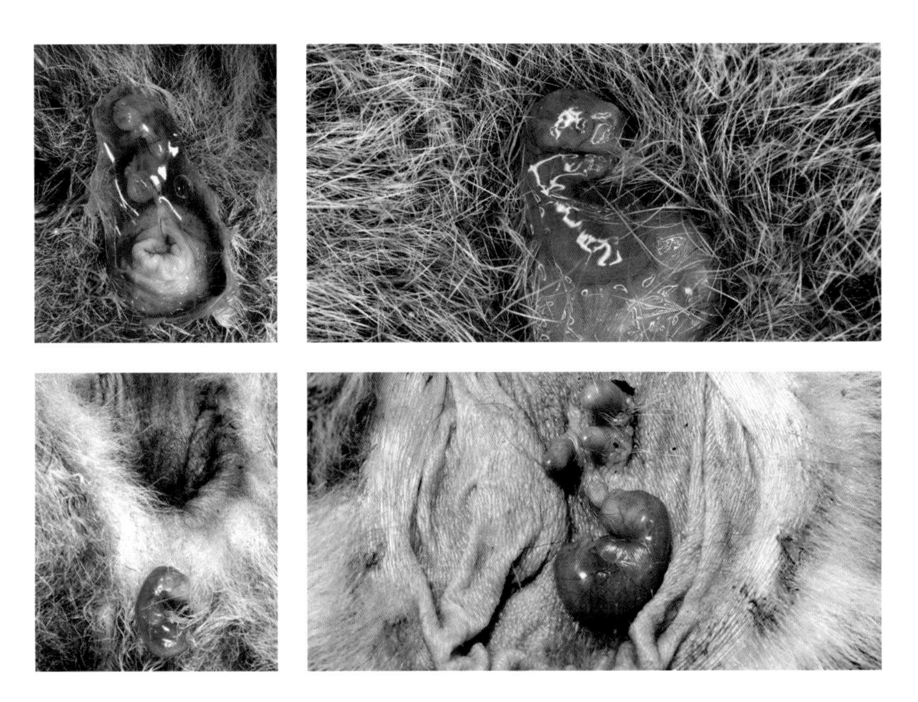

birthing & raising joey

Different macropod species have different gestation times, oestrous cycles and reproductive behaviour. Some are even able to control their reproduction to match the availability of food or water. This astonishing feat, known as "embryonic diapause", allows females to keep a tiny, undeveloped embryo (called a blastocyst) dormant during drought, or in case her pouch young dies. Under normal conditions, gestation takes between 31–36 days, after which a doe gives birth to an underdeveloped jelly bean-sized joey. This tiny embryo then begins an incredible climb to survival. Pulling itself unaided through the thick fur around its mother's cloaca, it makes its way to the pouch, where it attaches to a teat and begins to suckle.

OPPOSITE: A Red-necked Wallaby joey will start to leave the pouch when it is as young as six months old, although it will not venture far from its mother's side.
ABOVE: A Tammar Wallaby embryo tears through the foetal membrane (top) and starts its arduous climb to the pouch (above left) where it begins to feed (above right).

ABOVE: Western Grey joeys enjoy the creature comforts of the pouch for around nine months, but once they are fully furred they may occasionally hop out and begin to experience life "on the hop" outside.

ABOVE: Sometimes, if there is not a smaller sibling waiting in the wings to evict them, joeys (such as this young Red Kangaroo) may test the limits of maternal care and grow quite large before they consent to leave their cosy abode.

ABOVE: The pouch, or marsupium, provides excellent protection for immature macropods that are too small to outrun predators. Even when mum uses her tail as a brake to deftly execute a sharp turn — as this Eastern Grey is doing — the joey is in no danger of tumbling out. Muscles at the top of the pouch contract, like a drawstring bag, to hold her precious cargo safe inside. OPPOSITE, CLOCKWISE FROM TOP: Sure its cosy, but as the joey grows the pouch may get a little too snug for comfort! Joeys of many species begin to feel the squeeze — Eastern Grey Kangaroo; Black-footed Rock-wallaby, Red-necked Wallaby; Red Kangaroo; Whiptail Wallaby; Western Grey Kangaroo.

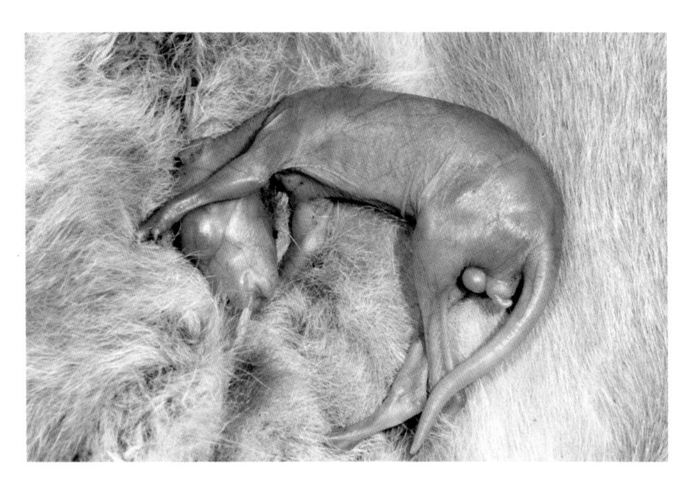

feeding joey

Joeys suckle in the pouch for around nine months before being booted out to make way for another big-footed baby. However, eviction from the pouch doesn't mean they must forgo mother's milk entirely. Female kangaroos and wallabies have four teats, enabling the pouch young to attach itself to one nipple while the young "at foot" occasionally pops in to drink from another. Such is the mother's suitability to this kind of offspring share arrangement, that she produces milk of two different kinds — one to nourish her unweaned joey and one to nourish her little one in the pouch. Kangaroo milk is very low in lactose, so special formulas are used to make milk for orphan joeys in human care.

OPPOSITE, CLOCKWISE FROM FAR LEFT: A Whiptail Wallaby joey takes a drink; Even while still drinking milk, a young Red-necked Wallaby imitates the herbivorous habits of its mother; A young Red-necked Pademelon explores other options on the menu. LEFT, TOP TO BOTTOM: Newborns suckle instinctively and continue to suckle and develop inside the pouch; When mother bends down to eat, a joey sometimes tries a nibble.

joeys on the jump

Maternal care continues for some time after the joey has left the pouch and it may be another nine months to more than a year before it is considered mature enough to make its own way in the world. Young males are then usually forced to form a mob, which isolates them from their mothers and female siblings. Each member of this little masculine band then strives to become a dominant buck leading a mob of his own.

OPPOSITE, LEFT TO RIGHT: Juvenile Whiptail Wallaby; A Red-necked Wallaby with her nearly independent offspring. BELOW: A junior Common Wallaroo tackles his mother.

OPPOSITE: Although a female Quokka may be carrying a furless joey in her pouch, she will also still care for the previous season's yearling. Quokkas exhibit considerable devotion to their young, which, being so small, are easily preyed upon. ABOVE: Once fully weaned and schooled — at approximately 18–24 months of age — a young Eastern Grey Kangaroo is big enough to fend for itself.

survival — a roo's perspective

Despite their exponential reproductive rate, species diversity and vast distribution across this continent, Australia's macropods cannot afford to be complacent about their survival. Nor, it seems, can we. In a little over 200 years of settlement, at least 20 of this continent's mammal species have been obliterated. Human habitation and hunting, the destruction of habitat and the introduction of feral predators are obstacles that some species, macropods among them, have been unable to overcome. Every day, kangaroos and wallabies and the more diminutive bettongs, potoroos and rat-kangaroos run the gauntlet of carnivorous predators including Wedge-tailed Eagles, Dingoes and, in the country's north, crocodiles. Although many species have strategies to combat drought, it continues to claim the lives of many joeys in arid regions. Australia's notoriously savage bushfires can also have a devastating impact on small species, especially those isolated by distance.

LEFT: Wedge-tailed Eagles are formidable predators of macropods. They can easily carry off a weaned joey.

ABOVE, TOP TO BOTTOM: Big feet provide little benefit when waterholes turn to muddy, quicksand-like bogs; Drought-stricken Common Wallaroos are even more vulnerable to attacks from hungry Wedge-tailed Eagles.

fire & drought

Fire is a natural — and essential — regime in the Australian bush. It encourages the regrowth of fresh grass and the replenishment of some floral species, but for many macropods a bushfire can be a death sentence. Larger, more fleet of foot species can sometimes outrun a blaze, but smaller grassland species, with nowhere to run and few places to hide, can perish rapidly. Those individuals that do survive the flames often succumb to famine or infection caused by burns. The relentless, scorching heat of drought can have a similar effect, causing joeys and adults to die by the hundreds as waterholes become boggy or vanish entirely.

ABOVE: Surrounded by flames, an Eastern Grey Kangaroo makes a swift escape from an advancing bushfire.

TOP: In Australia's tropical north and interior, feral pigs cause damage to the grassy edges around billabongs and floodplains, areas favoured by grazing macropods. BOTTOM, LEFT AND RIGHT: Carnivorous feral cats, foxes and rats have contributed greatly to Australia's record rate of mammal extinction and, along with habitat destruction and human hunting, are primary causes of the extinction of six macropod species since European settlement. Unfortunately, feral predators are notoriously difficult to eradicate.

feral

predators & competitors

European settlers introduced more problems than they could have imagined when they brought non-native species onto this continent. Some fragile habitats, unsuited to the cloven feet and voracious grazing habits of feral goats and donkeys, now struggle to support native animals that are perfectly adapted to Australian ecosystems. More insidious species were also released — some, like the Red Fox, were introduced purely for sport and have caused serious damage to smaller macropod, potoroo and bettong populations.

ABOVE: Wild donkeys and brumbies destroy prime habitat with their hard hooves and intensive grazing. According to the Federal Government there are an estimated 300,000 feral horses and over five million donkeys running wild in Australia.

native predators

Invaders from other continents are not the only threats macropods face. Evolution often favours the bold, hence the emergence of native carnivores to help keep macropod species in check. The rapacious Wedge-tailed Eagle swoops down on weak animals and will abduct and devour healthy joeys if left unattended. Dingoes — considered Australia's native dog species, despite being introduced by South-East Asian traders around 5000 years ago — are canny, savage hunters that make many a meal of kangaroos, wallabies and small macropod species. Joeys, potoroos, bettongs and small wallaby species can also make a stomach-bulging feast for large pythons.

ABOVE, LEFT TO RIGHT: During drought or famine, even large Red Kangaroos are susceptible to attack by Wedge-tailed Eagles; Dingoes are swift and wily carnivores with the stamina to chase down (or the smarts to ambush) Swamp Wallabies and other species. OPPOSITE: Although enormous, this Olive Python faces quite a task consuming and digesting this wallaroo carcass.

OPPOSITE, TOP TO BOTTOM: The Tasmanian Devil has an acute sense of smell — a dead or dying macropod or a joey separated from its mother will most certainly provide a meal. Even roadkill, such as this Swamp Wallaby, will be devoured by hungry Tasmanian Devil cubs; A Perentie, the largest goanna species in Australia, makes a tasty meal of a Burrowing Bettong. Unfortunately for the bettong, hiding in a burrow makes the Perentie's task all the more easy. ABOVE: Estuarine Crocodiles in the freshwater rivers and wetlands of northern Australia will not hesitate to snatch a drinking kangaroo. This crocodile has made short work of an Antilopine Wallaroo.

ABOVE: Kangaroos cannot be farmed in Australia, thus preserving their ranging lifestyles and wild quality of life. Commercial culling, although unfortunate for individual roos, is in the best interest of species that routinely grow to plague-like proportions. All macropod species are protected by law and only four roo species and one wallaby species can be harvested to strict quotas.

ABOVE: The slaughter of native fauna may seem cold-hearted, but a mitigating factor is that professional shooters kill quickly and humanely and use as much of an animal's carcass as possible. Meat, fur and skins are exported to 21 countries around the world.

the kangaroo industry

National icons they may be, but when conditions are good, prolific breeding can turn roos into pests in some parts of the country. There has been much conjecture over the best way to control rampant roo numbers, and the commercial kangaroo industry is one way of limiting populations of common macropod species. One thing is beyond argument — over-population causes habitat degradation and mass starvation. Hence, keeping numbers at a sustainable level is within the best interests of native species. Licensed shooters abide by a National Code of Practice for the Humane Killing of Kangaroos, harvesting kangaroos to strict annual quotas under the auspices of the Federal *Environment Protection and Biodiversity Conservation Act 1999*. Peak animal welfare bodies in Australia, such as the RSPCA have conceded that: "If achieved correctly, kangaroo culling is considered one of the most humane forms of animal slaughter".

home on the farm

Agricultural practices have done little to limit abundant kangaroo populations and much to encourage them. Roos make the most of well-irrigated crop fields and may also help themselves to stock feed troughs and "licks". They also benefit from dam water provided in previously dehydrated areas. Most fences, unless specifically designed to keep roos and Dingoes out, are easily negotiated by all but the smallest species. Macropods are protected by law, so most hobby and crop farmers tolerate their presence, shooing away large mobs and often cursing their tenacity; others may even have "pet" kangaroos at home on the farm.

OPPOSITE, TOP TO BOTTOM: Crops prove irresistible for kangaroos in climates where little other vegetation is maintained during dry times; Red Kangaroos are familiar visitors to homesteads in Australia's Outback. ABOVE: Stock troughs quench the thirst of kangaroos and wallaroos in areas otherwise devoid of water.

NEXT
30 km

roads & roo bars

Anyone who has travelled the continent's outback roads knows that cars and road trains are the scourge of roo species. Carcasses litter Australia's inland highways, with dead females attended by orphaned joeys — the infant casualties of roadkill. When blinded by headlights, macropods are very unpredictable, so swerving to avoid a bounding "roo roadblock" can prove fatal for both macropod and humans, especially on gravel roads. Hefty Red Kangaroos, greys and wallaroos can inflict considerable damage upon vehicles, prompting many motorists to install sturdy "roo bars" to minimise damage to their cars. Roo bars have an awful impact on the roos, and many companies have experimented with devices that emit high-pitched sounds to keep roos away from roads — a far better option for both roos and motorists.

OPPOSITE: Signs punctuate Australia's inland roads, warning motorists of potential "roo crossings". ABOVE, LEFT TO RIGHT: A Red Kangaroo dices with death; People who kill or maim a roo on the road should always stop to check for a joey that may have survived. Joeys should be taken to a vet or wildlife organisation, and WIRES (Wildlife Information and Rescue Education Service, phone 1300 094 737) alerted.

habitat destruction

In the heyday of European settlement we often did not know or care enough about our habitats or our fauna to recognise the likely impact of effectively pulling the land out from under the macropods' feet. Burning and bulldozing vast tracts of land across a range of habitats for the purpose of agriculture or development, and introducing rabbits and domestic stock (which deplete habitats of minerals and essential plant communities), compounded our environmental woes and contributed to Australia's unnecessary extinctions.

OPPOSITE, TOP TO BOTTOM: Rabbits destroy native habitats across the country; Urban sprawl has caused considerable conflict between macropods and people. ABOVE: An ill-advised, human-centric approach to "development" and habitat destruction has been one of the major factors in Australian marsupial extinction.

kangaroo
care & conservation

Paradoxically, our existence is both a hindrance and a help to wild creatures. We run down the roo, but save its immature joey and nurture it with a protectiveness akin to parenthood. We eat our national icon, yet preserve it in country-wide parks and reserves. We embrace the wonders of the wild and revere nature, yet our burgeoning population remains one of nature's greatest threats. Dealing with this paradox requires us to educate ourselves and our children about how to best live in harmony with other species and serve their interests as well as our own.

However, the media invariably presents us with the doom and gloom of environmental mismanagement, which can numb some people into a sense of hopelessness. We rarely, if ever, hear the good news stories that raise our spirits and present us with hope. There are many good news stories about macropods, such as the rediscovery of the Gilbert's Potoroo and the many successful re-introductions of macropods from reserves back into the wild undertaken by the Australian Wildlife Conservancy and other conservation organisations. Grass-roots groups and wildlife carers also help nurture injured or orphaned macropods, volunteering their own time and resources to rescue and rehabilitate native wildlife before reintroducing them back to the wild — a demanding but rewarding commitment.

OPPOSITE: The Brush-tailed Rock-wallaby, which is vulnerable to extinction in Queensland, is protected here in Crows Nest National Park on the Great Dividing Range west of Brisbane. LEFT: At Currumbin Sanctuary on the Gold Coast, wildlife carers do an excellent job of conserving wildlife and educating people about Australia's native animals.

"Even though an encounter with a wild animal may be brief, its effect on the human spirit can last a lifetime."

I hope this book inspired you and impassioned your intention to connect with nature, to think about conservation of our wild species, and to form your own lifelong love affair with Australia's macropod fauna. — STEVE PARISH

Distribution of Australian kangaroos and their relatives

Potoroos

Long-footed Potoroo

Long-nosed Potoroo

Gilbert's Potoroo

Bettongs & Musky Rat-kangaroo

Northern Bettong

Rufous Bettong

Southern Bettong

Burrowing Bettong

Brush-tailed Bettong

Musky Rat-kangaroo

Hare-wallabies

Spectacled Hare-wallaby

Rufous Hare-wallaby

Banded Hare-wallaby

Pademelons

Tasmanian Pademelon

Red-legged Pademelon

Red-necked Pademelon

Tree-kangaroos

Bennett's Tree-kangaroo

Lumholtz's Tree-kangaroo

Quokka

Quokka

Rock-wallabies

Yellow-footed Rock-wallaby

Brush-tailed Rock-wallaby

Short-eared Rock-wallaby

Monjon

Nabarlek

Black-footed Rock-wallaby

Purple-necked Rock-wallaby

Rothschild's Rock-wallaby

North-eastern Queensland Rock-wallabies

Proserpine Rock-wallaby

Mareeba Rock-wallaby

Allied Rock-wallaby

Cape York Rock-wallaby

Godman's Rock-wallaby

Sharman's Rock-wallaby

Herbert's Rock-wallaby

Unadorned Rock-wallaby

Swamp Wallaby

Swamp Wallaby

Nailtail Wallabies

Bridled Nailtail Wallaby

Northern Nailtail Wallaby

Typical Wallabies

Agile Wallaby

Black-striped Wallaby

Tammar Wallaby

Western Brush Wallaby

Parma Wallaby

Whiptail Wallaby

Red-necked Wallaby

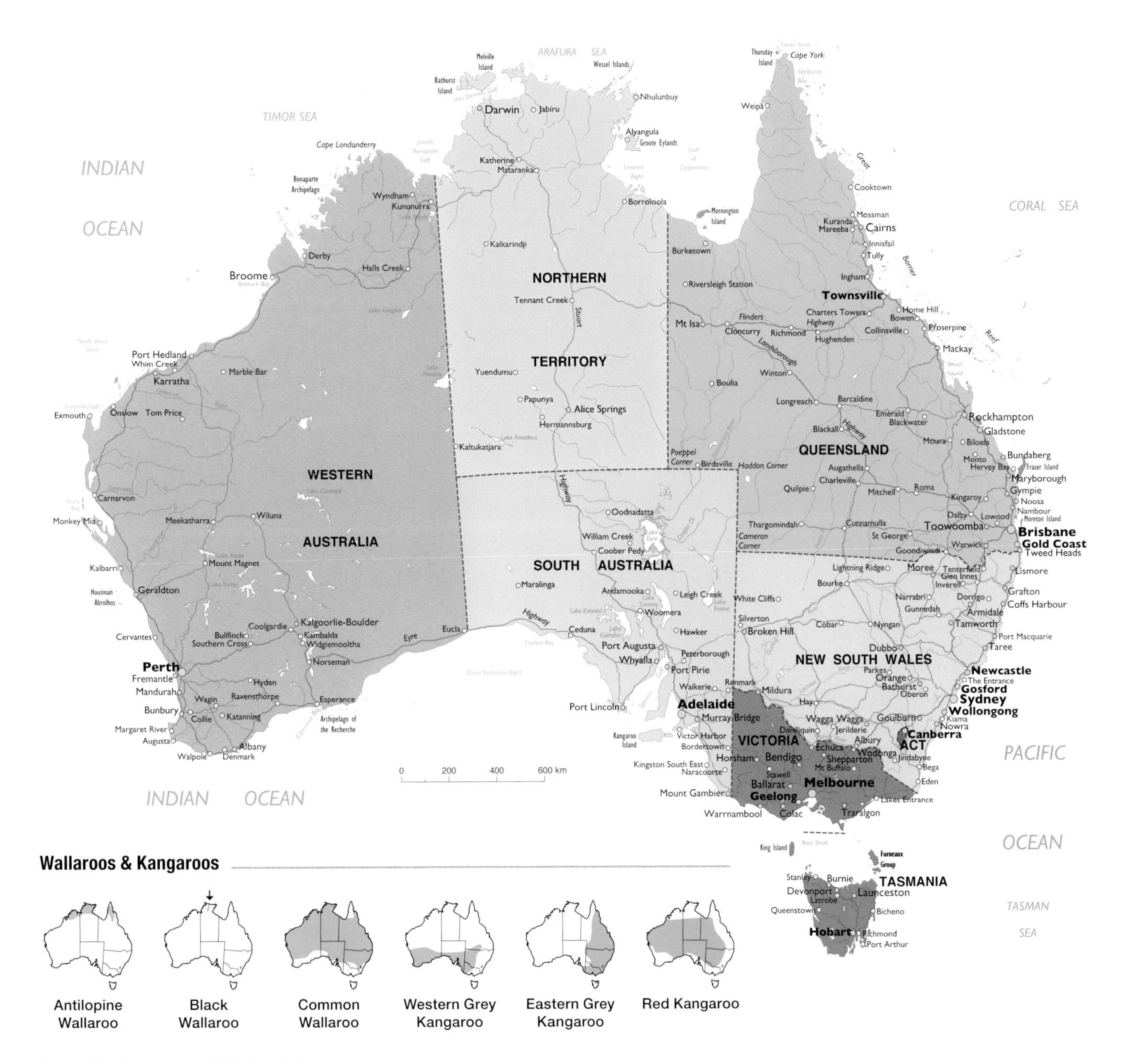

Australian kangaroos & their relatives

Fifty macropod species inhabit the Australian mainland and/or adjacent islands. This book features all species except the Sharman's, Herbert's, Godman's and Cape York Rock-wallabies, each of which is considered visually identical to the Allied, Unadorned and Mareeba Rock-wallabies; in fact, the only sure way to tell them apart is by DNA testing. Before European settlement, a further six species existed — these are now extinct. Even today, many of the macropods featured in this book are listed as rare or endangered, particularly the smaller rock-wallabies, hare-wallabies, bettongs and potoroos.

index

Acknowledgements

A big thank you to Damian McGreevy who first introduced me to these wonderful animals in the wilds of Bulloo, South-East Queensland, in 1975. Ian Morris's keen eye and in-depth knowledge of macropods, particularly the shy tropical varieties, has also been a major inspiration. Although my encounters with Peter Johnson and "his" rock-wallabies have been brief, his enthusiasm and dedication to these shy and agile creatures has long simmered in my spirit. Thanks also to the photographers listed below, whose images contributed to the telling of this story.

Thanks to my many associates who work with and care for macropods in Australia's zoos, national parks, reserves and fauna parks. These people have granted me close physical contact with macropods, which has been essential for making many of the images in this book. Finally, I would like to commend the tireless efforts of the staff of the Australian Wildlife Conservancy — for their conservation work and also for creating opportunities for me to photograph many species that would simply disappear if it were not for their commitment.

Steve Parish Publishing Pty Ltd
PO Box 1058, Archerfield, Qld 4108 Australia

Photography: Steve Parish.

Additional photography: Tony Allingham/ANTPhoto.com: p. 98; Jack Cameron/ANTPhoto.com: pp. 10, 133 & 136 (top); Pavel German/ANTPhoto.com: p. 138 (bottom left); Martin Harvey/ANTPhoto.com: pp. 22-3 & 37 (top right); Tony Howard/ANTPhoto.com: p. 106; Ford Kristo/ANTPhoto.com: pp. 134-5 & 148; Fredy Mercay: p. 26 (centre); Frank Park/ANTPhoto.com: p. 19 (right); Otto Rogge/ANTPhoto.com: p. 131; Rik Thwaites/ANTPhoto.com: p. 11; Dave Watts/ANTPhoto.com: pp. 32 (bottom left), 52-3, 89 (top), 92 & 120-1; Dick Whitford/ANTPhoto.com: p. 149 (right); Theo Allofs/Auscape: p. 107; Nicholas Birks/Auscape: p. 94; John Cancalosi/Auscape: pp. 93 & 112; Jean-Paul Ferrero/Auscape: pp. 70-1, 114, 123 (bottom left), 124, 144 & 145; Ferrero-Labat/Auscape: p. 102 (left); Wayne Lawler/Auscape: p. 27 (right); D. Parer & E. Parer-Cook/Auscape: pp. 113 & 123 (top left & right, and bottom right); Michael Cermak: p. 95; Graeme Chapman: pp. 138 (top) & 150 (top); Greg Harm: p. 63; Bill Belson/Lochman Transparencies: p. 155; Hans & Judy Beste/Lochman Transparencies: pp. 29 (bottom left), 89 (bottom) & 154; Jiri Lochman/Lochman Transparencies: pp. 26 (bottom left & right), 30 (bottom), 99, 129 (top), 142 (bottom) & 150 (bottom); Marie Lochman/Lochman Transparencies: p. 61 (centre); Len Stewart/Lochman Transparencies: p. 18; Dave Watts/Lochman Transparencies: pp. 32 (bottom right) & 56 (bottom); M & I Morcombe: pp. 34 (bottom), 88 & 140 (left); Ian Morris: pp. 8, 26 (top left & bottom centre), 28 (left), 32 (top left), 54-5, 54 (bottom), 59, 78, 80, 96, 100 (top), 115, 141 & 143; Gary Cranitch/Queensland Museum: p. 44 (right); Gary Steer: p. 142 (top)

Illustrations: John Gould: pp. 29 (top right), 31, 33, 35, 43

Text: Karin Cox, SPP

Design: Leanne Nobilio, SPP

Editorial: Ted Lewis, Mary Ann Ghaffurian & Michele Perry SPP; Britt Winter

Production: Wendy Mansell, SPP

First published 2007
ISBN: 978174193282 9

Prepress by Colour Chiefs Digital Imaging, Brisbane, Australia
Printed in China by Everbest Printing Co Ltd.

Produced in Australia at the Steve Parish Publishing Studios

FRONT COVER: **Red Kangaroo.** ABOVE, TOP AND BOTTOM: **Juvenile Red Kangaroo.** BACK COVER: **Female Western Brush Wallaby.**